This Book Belongs To:

Printed in Great Britain
by Amazon

64063842R00066